T0161368

GLASS ARMONICA

GLASS ARMONICA

REBECCA DUNHAM

poems

MILKWEED EDITIONS

Published 2013 by Milkweed Editions
Printed in Canada
Cover design by Gretchen Achilles/Wavetrap Design
Author photo by Mark Pioli

13 14 15 16 17   5 4 3 2 1
First Edition

Milkweed Editions, an independent nonprofit publisher, gratefully acknowledges
sustaining support from the Bush Foundation; the Patrick and Aimee Butler Foundation;
the Dougherty Family Foundation; the Driscoll Foundation; the Jerome Foundation;
the Lindquist & Vennum Foundation; the McKnight Foundation; the voters of Minnesota
through a Minnesota State Arts Board Operating Support grant, thanks to a legislative
appropriation from the arts and cultural heritage fund, and a grant from the Wells Fargo
Foundation Minnesota; the National Endowment for the Arts; the Target Foundation;
and other generous contributions from foundations, corporations, and individuals.
For a full listing of Milkweed Editions supporters, please visit www.milkweed.org.

Library of Congress Cataloging-in-Publication Data

Dunham, Rebecca, 1973–
[Poems. Selections]
Glass Armonica : Poems / Rebecca Dunham.
pages   cm
Summary: "In these poems, Dunham probes the depths of human psyche, inhabiting the
voices of historical female "hysterics" and offering a portrait of the female body in the act of
being touched"—Provided by publisher.
ISBN 978-1-57131-466-6 (pbk.)—ISBN 978-1-57131-913-5 (e-book)
I. Title.
PS3604.U54A6 2013
811'.6—dc23
2013026959

Milkweed Editions is committed to ecological stewardship. We strive to align our book pro-
duction practices with this principle, and to reduce the impact of our operations in the
environment. We are a member of the Green Press Initiative, a nonprofit coalition of
publishers, manufacturers, and authors working to protect the world's endangered
forests and conserve natural resources. *Glass Armonica* was printed on
acid-free 100% postconsumer-waste paper by the Friesens Corporation.

for

Dorothy and Fern

for

Janet and Anna

CONTENTS

~

~

SELF-PORTRAIT AS GALLERY

~

. . . What took me
completely by surprise
was that it was me:
my voice, in my mouth . . .

I scarcely dared to look
to see what it was I was.

ELIZABETH BISHOP

GLASS ARMONICA

REBECCA

after the novel by Daphne du Maurier

Counter the clock: let its hands whir hot as a circular saw.
The dead do return to stalk their familiar halls — scent of
crushed azalea, lipsticked cloth fished from a mackintosh
pocket. Fast and blue, I pour cyclonic, the kind of knowledge
a husband would keep for himself: pleasures of the flesh,
peat-smoked whiskey's steady burn, and the certainty one
will win in the end. It is worth it — bullet to the heart, spike-
drilled hull, the sea cocks left open and rushing. Remember:
Rebecca did this, as I am doing, and put the lily to the vase's
open mouth, *not the first to do it.*

To the fruit

Rose-soaked ovoid rising like
sun leak on peach skin:
>   pyramids arranged in grocery

bins fluoresce, saying *press one*, *test one* —
it will pass its examination,
such adolescent flesh — it will pass —

but dark-ridged is the pit
>   that lies in wait within.

*

In the observatory

Jupiter's red eye stares us down
through the centuries: *never subside*,

       its lush, telescoped form
whispers to my refracted gaze. Its shifty
storm seems invulnerable
to the fermentation of time —
                it does not know what

my mirror shows, the body I face
off against each day.

    *

Verses on death

*where are the beautiful
women, the splendid cities of long ago?*
O Hélinand of Froidmont —

all has vanished

*

To the body dysmorphic

Not my own figure in the glass, but
the crone's

I will become, an abomination,
a symbol of decay —
                    I watch the pale worms

pierce her sternum. And then
there are the flies . . .

serpents straitjacket her arms
and her pubis is made
                    decent not by fig leaf but aubergine

toad:
she is no green petal.

A piece of coffee

Coffee: of the madder family. And what
of my own? We're mad as any beans that click
in the bin. My baby girl shakes her toy rattle,
    pill-bottle brown.

A red stamp

A little lip, pocketed, hid in his pants,
teeth shredding the slick lining to a satin nest.
This tattooed corsage, a blistering, and me?
    Return to sender.

Water raining

Her hands folding, unfolding. Arms like a bolt
cutter. Ashes, ashes, on her tongue. And she
already knows how it ends. Gin ribbons
    tonic. All fall down.

A little bit of a tumbler

The kidney-shaped plastic dish, an entire
pharmacy of pills, and me, charcoaled. Like an ex-
starlet's pool in algae-bloom. Like this is what will
      teach me my lesson.

A paper

Never write out of anger, pencil staking
the breast, whip-stitched and wound tight as a murder
in police tape. Unhand her, I say. A ribbon
      hit, repeatedly.

A cutlet

He stalks me. An antlered basilisk, he writes
knife-notes, odes to a slit testicle's white moon.
Oh my dear girl, he likes to say, *what a nice
      piece of meat you'll make.*

More

Heave ho. There really is a bowl for every
occasion. Don your best hospital gown and
haul death up, a gizzard. It's someone else's
job to clean it.

The stop-watched tick. The seconds enough
to reckon, to weigh. The pill a pillow pressed to —

Just a swine flu of the mind, just a little touch, I confess
to a waiting room of lips masked clean shut.

If to bandage is to veil, and to veil is to disguise,
then we must learn to bind our purblind eyes.

Like a grave rubbing, the midwives press paper
to my cauled face, sailor's charm, *half-a-crown a head.*

Cover your mouth, Rebecca, the patients' blue-
papered jaws crinkle at me. *Just a little. Just a touch.*

Face covered by the long
sterile drape, I could be anyone.
This will make it easier,
he thinks. He drills, stippling

a semi-circle across my shorn
scalp and peels the dura free
in flaps. How can I survive?
The doctors say things like

plasticity. Then each one
shrugs, admits: *We don't really
know*. But my body has already
held a vacancy as deep as this

entire hemisphere, revealed.
If the mind is the soul's seat,
then the brain must be
its dwelling: the doctor lifts it

tenderly, lobe by lobe
from my opened skull's wide
uneven bowl, an infant
who is bound to disappoint.

GLASS ARMONICA

List of all I can recall: his hair,
red and curly; I was ten; how I slept
in the top bunk, in July heat;
his first name: Richard;

damp-swollen smell of pine
and unwashed clothes in the girls'
cabin; waking to his hand;
the camp director forbid the piercing

of each others' ears — we'd catch
lockjaw — ; leg-stroke; fingers
against a sleeping bag's clenched steel
seam; my friend Prue; the lawyer's

call; our family room; my parents
asking me to tell them what I knew.

They asked us to tell them
the truth — there was proof — girls'
photos recovered from his trash;
our names and dates noted
meticulous in his little black book.
We were safe. But all of our jaws
were locked. We knew nothing
about all of that. Did not recall
those days in the infirmary,
Prue and I holding thermometer to
lightbulb, nor the inexplicable way
our eyes crossed and limbs shook.
The nurse never told. We were
homesick. We were good patients.

Mary Glover in London, 1602

I am sick, the doctors say, and offer
to count the ways. They call it
affliction of the uterus, the *globus*
hystericus. I call it 'clod of cold
porridge lodged in the throat.' I call it
the devil and no tight lacing or
birdseed diet can exorcise that grip.
I name my tormentor, and though
I cannot speak, still the voice box tics
and creaks: *Hange, Hange* —
I turn *round as a whoope, heade back*
to hippes. They testify to the womb's
wandering. How it constricts. Dear sirs,
don't you think I'd know it if it did?

Don't kid yourself. You don't know
what crouches, seething, under
lock and key. An infestation:
a dozen for every one you see, hiding,
tunneling —   I was ten.
Prue's mother insisted she could hear
them chewing. They opened
the wall to a colony of carpenter ants

frothing in bulbous-black ropes.
Myrmecophobia: fear of ants. Due, I am
told, to another memory I do not
recall: an explosion of tiny ants rivering
my hands when I snapped
the doll's head free from her neck.

—for Prue

You're a doll, her father says. She is
helpful, she smiles, she is not
bound for the doll hospital. Moors
ball-jointed limbs into place. Ask
not what nests inside her head,
dried apple balanced
on an effigy's stuffed rag-flesh.
She cannot say. She casts spells
upon herself, a child's poppet
pierced by pins. Here.
And here. The therapist lays the naked
doll in her hands. *Where?*
he asks. She schools her face.
          Was it here? Or here? Or here?

Augustine, at the Salpêtrière, 1875

There, there, Charcot presses, *oh dear*
love, dear Augustine. I belong to his
unique body of cure: 1) of ether:
"That's how you make babies," he says
I say, as I *gently sway legs and pelvis*;
2) of tuning fork: I speak of men
as *beasts like big rats* and *when they*
speak, flames emerge from their mouths.

The photographer catches it —
How my *physiognomy expresses regret* . . .
Abundant vaginal secretion. Speculum,
a doctor pushing his long needle into
my exposed neck, and how I smile
for the camera, a *knowing* smile (he says).

. . . the girls know things — flash's
blink — eclipse on an eyelid's
    convex screen — they buried
the bodies out back, stiff
    limbed — his images stacked
and shuffled like a flipbook
    in the prosecutor's hands — it was
Prue's shoebox that coffined
    the four broken dolls — found
in his building's public bin —
    beneath the shifting bush — the girls
refuse to recall the exact spot —
    all soil-mooned nails and pulsing
shiver of each beetle-plagued leaf.

Franz Mesmer, Vienna, 1877

She shivers like a leaf in easy wind
at the passing of my hands
above her skin — I never quite touch —
Still, she's drawn to me, filings
to my magnet. I imagine her fingers
beneath mine like ivory
keys, listen as she respires a lavender
crush. I urge her to put

aside this hysteria and play her
like a glass armonica, pull tone upon
tone from her, for hours.
Then I withdraw, brush my iron rod
along the fainting sofa's back,
and she opens her blind eyes, and sees.

I sleep open-eyed. Not
because I am afraid, at least no more
than a child fears the gable in winter,
its guttered jaw of ice-

impacted teeth. No, I do not fear
the hasped door, the hairdryer's roar,
nor worry that they deaden
the approach of footfalls in the hall.

After all, I am not the only one
who doesn't like a surprise, who won't
watch that movie with its girl
and her button eyes.

The horror is not the sewing on.
The horror is who will unfasten you.

To unfasten, to unbed trauma
from memory's sediment, the doctors
tried setons, tried leeches
and purges, ovarian compression,
then pills — all manner of pills —
opiates, iron, strychnine, quinine,
mercury, pills to produce
vomits, laxatives, and then

there were the other remedies —
bleedings by lancet,
by razor to leg, thorazine,
fluoxetine, the starvation diets
and hypnotic trance, until the hysteric
curled (good girl) at their feet.

At my feet, pine's curled shavings —
And its sound, too, whine of the planer
in shop class. I was thirteen.
Gleaming knots. Ribboned wood.

Like a mind smoothed down to size.
That was the year I cut my hair
and let all the locks fall,
blond feathers haloing our sink.

Work with the grain, my teacher said,
not against. But how to shear
the feel of their hands from my flesh?
Go with the flow, my mother said.

A perfect blank. *If you can't
say something nice, don't say anything at all.*

"Charcot Presents the Hysteric," André Brouillet, 1887

Her audience says nothing. Just watches:
like petal from stamen, she arcs
back, draped over his assistant's arm—
Blanche Whitman performs the *attitude*

passionelle, the state of *extase* that marks
the third stage of Charcot's *grand*
hystérie. Pelvis thrust forward, her breasts
tease the blouse's neck, and the crowd

leans forward for a better look.
In the name of science. Torso torqued,
she swoons, stilled and then spun,
distillate to their liquored gaze.

Her body: oiled and framed, then
hooked and hung on Freud's office wall.

In the end, the pictures were enough
to hang him. My red-haired man
weighed, locked away — found wanting.
Now I am supposed to tell you how
I don't hate men. Bitterness is so
unbecoming. Confession: behind
each man I meet stretches a never-ending
rope, figures on an assembly line.

Confession: I want to pack them up, bind
necks and arms with wire twist-ties.
I call this justice. For the doctor, I unpeel
myself — derma flayed — and point. *See?*
See under growth's choke, its roots? He calls it
delusion, says it has only to do with me.

Augustine, at the Salpêtrière, September 1880

Call it delusion, but it is one I have
practiced, repeatingly, charm to resurrect
Eve's knowledge, to lay claim to
Adam's rib as my own. List of all I can
recall: razor to my neck, my mother's
lover devouring me. I was ten. I was
thirteen. Charcot's notes: *she looks almost
like a full-grown woman.* Indeed, the men
of my neighborhood agreed. Seized,
each spell is reenactment, is rehearsal.
I play both roles in turn: push myself
down, *arc-en-cercle*, rip my own gown free.
A release. How else to flee Salpêtrière
but as a man, to set my skin unkeyed —

THE GARDEN OF EARTHLY DELIGHTS

after the triptych by Hieronymous Bosch

1. Paradise

Fowl and beast skirt our feet.
I float sexless —

porcelain doll
with eyes that open

and close. Please,
no half-swallowed frog,

legs pitch-forked
and helpless

in some bird's unnatural
mouth, no

feral cat's
dangle-jawed mouse.

This hunger, his gift to us —
the animal appetites

as yet unnamed, our own
still unacknowledged.

Songbirds spiral
and swarm like bees

smoked from a honeyed
hive. A warning.

2. Fallen

Rose-bellied finches
larger than man.
Eyes like a damson stone.

Stripped bare
and plumed emergency-
bright, my lips

feather and fledge.

The egg's open skull a bed
wide enough for all.

Rinse my palate
— mouth-deep in red —

strawberries
swollen to the exact
size of my desire.

Hip to hip,
be it fish or fowl, be it
man or beast —

the body
does not discriminate.

3. Hell

strung and luted spread your legs

what goes in must come out

the banquet table *en flambé*

stomach plattered and pink

a knife a rattle a long, hard hiss

consumption a torso carved

the bird-man takes another

— ah, the slings and arrows —

canapé: you and your frog-legs

beneath the throne — the pit

rose-sore :: eros
and rill :: the land
tortured :: true
my pretty pretty :: pet
watered :: red wet
germinate :: in rime
my :: hymen my
mons :: no
stiletto :: let slit
wheal awl :: hew all
predator :: or parade
pressed to :: bed
a body :: abode
seeded :: spread
chenille :: to lichen
to her to her :: to other

Knife

What flies, air halved
a-hiss, metal
ringing and ringing its silver
bell — each line a flash
that strobes the mind,
a chain of arrow-
heads strung and hung about
R's neck —

*

Mother is egg is swollen
to breaking. Can't see
her feet. Can't see R's
toy plane, its steel arrow.

She trips to the floor, linseed-
oiled, orange squares.

*

It is as if His metatarsal
can comb her
mind's curled whites,
buds nested and wet —
whittling this from that,
R's mind a split
melon cut and scooped.

*

His fingers scratch R's back,
deer's teeth against tree-
bark in winter, peeling spine
bare and white and hanging
in shreds this physic of mind.

*

R:

Orange vial, its mass
of white clouds, how they tap,
(do I mind?) a bell-clapper, against
its throat and mine.

Redux

linseed orange flies breaking
curled finger buds
an arrow bell-white tap
claps R's mindstrings spined
flesh flash halved

as bloodroot,
bundled vascular and impervious

to the trowel, to the chemical
bath, to the plastic

pulled over it in sheets —
        it will not be expelled.

I close my eyes. The rotary tiller's
engine is a shell held to the ear,

its hot breath an insistent
sussuration: *persist, persist*

Not beauty. Not the milkweed's
orbed catch of petals but

jeweled pestilence, ravaging need
— its strange and sudden

                promise: hard
rain of black amid the grass,

fistful after fistful of wedding rice.

The good, thick wool of it.

Whorl of ointment.
The bandage lovingly applied.

Come, night. Come, sleep.
Come, fog, wreathed in feather·
and sift. My face
cast impassive as a queen.

The cut white moon.

The selfsame body beside me
in bed, so sweet
and still I could die for her.

Ice-drift
and near-miss in early morning traffic.

My palm like a crumpled kiss.

SELF-PORTRAIT AS GALLERY

SELF-PORTRAIT AS CONVULSION

as Lavinia Dickinson and her Daisy

Hands out, she flails, blind
to fall's chloral leaves as they flurry
a silver snow. My mind's stutter

a galaxy caught mid-spin and cast
carelessly back. Unfaced, I am
moon-black and still, pillow in hand,

culpable as night's skirt enfolds
my sister's form. I want
to lay down with her, immobile,

and let heaven flay me, field
of loosestrife threshed to a fine flame.
Sweat's purled scent washes

my brow as I throw my spirit
supine through the library's half-
open door. Skull seized

and portioned orange bright, I braid
her fingers and mine. We leap
as one, into morning's nacred light.

SELF-PORTRAIT AS FRAGMENT

as "Dora" to Sigmund Freud

I am the good stenographer.
My fingers tap out
thoughts upon my thighs
before they cross my lips' lush
seam. You say the first
account is an unnavigable
river. I say, stream choked
by mass of rock. Say,
do Herr K. yourself. Divided,
then lost. Come beautiful
as a wind-whipped and blooded
white sheet. Amid shallow
and bank, become over-
come. Volt of hysteria jag me,
zigzagged and holy — I
will not unravel: O, pinking
shears. O sawtoothed one.

Persona: Latin for theatrical mask, from the masked Etruscan
gladiator, Tomb of the Augurs, 6ᵗʰ c. BC

1.

I am the mask, the face
        I wear red and serpent-
like as the leash I hold.
        My false beard and cap
peaked as the saw
        palmetto plant.
Your face: shrouded and sacked
        in rough linen, its flesh
opening beneath my dog's
        feral teeth —
how whitely bared and ripping.

2.

All men are cowards.
You are proof of this — your features
veiled as those of the condemned
at their execution. Don't you see?
They fear you more than my counterfeit
face, your live flesh made mask,
stiff and fixed in rictus of death.

3.

Blood foams.
      Hobbled by my long
looped cord, you will fall
to my feet. You always do.

It would be no fun if you didn't
fight. You could not know
        your club is mere outline,
pencil-thin and half-erased —

4.

At root, in the end, all you are is mask.
The living prefer disguise,
the bivalve's hinged shell shutting
over its vulnerable flesh. But this mask
was made to consume, not unlike
the Greeks who swallowed my name
and let it slide cool down their throats
before voicing it anew.

Pluck me, liar, and I'll sing to you

The hollow of my throat
is silver moan, is crescent sharp

Fall's chorus of *aught, knot, ought,
naught* — tie me in nots —

Tonight I will drape morning's
pinesweet blacks about me

Tonight I will release and finger-
comb the furrows of my hair

Tonight I am both bridaled
and casked   Your wants mill me

pollen-gold and fine   You reap
me, an unlit field, your thirst

a press that leaves behind only
skin   I drink the rape-wine

Your fingers dowse each rich seam

after a line by Cato the Elder

Let Carthage fall. Salt both
soil and city street alike. He said
some things are meant to be
destroyed. It is a calculation,
deliberate pouring. She told him
of lips burned black and peeling.
He promised to cover her
like dirt on a coffin. She vowed
lines of muddy divots, opening
like punctured mouths in their wake.
He said: I, too, have foreseen
such brutality and it is good.
They agreed: to place one's hands
on a stranger's skull is the most
erotic thing in the world.
She said: I will hand you the spade.

Feed me to myself.

Pleat and riddle the channels
of my mind, meal of bone and brain
           before me.

I will be as a God, bovine-mad
and felled in a wild rage.

The autoclave cannot break me.

I will speak in my own tongues,
will survive the culling,
           will persist here in pieces,

in patient soil and await the blade
that splits the humus dark —

I will rise, tasseled grain, in waves
of sunlight like sunlight
           folded in upon itself.

The soul is a sponge.

It can take so much, so boiling
and bright, it makes the eye ache.

LINES WRITTEN

ON THE MARGIN OF MY BOOK

Whip-sting of order —
the neighbor's electric
fence bares its lip, strip of dirt
dog-eared and worn.

Speech's scratched pencil.
A roach's static hiss.
Unbodied — my voice —
vacant strand the tape awaits.

Selvage — the outer rim
of a dragonfly's wing —
a space for error, a brink.
A respite from

the black-cragged throat:
this mute peninsula

LEARNING TO PRAY

for my teachers

1.

This emptiness — the body — means very little;

       scumble of lead white, coal soot
and the shadows they make together.

One time I rose to the ceiling. I closed like
a knife, hanging like flesh from the flame trees —

The lake claimed my arms and ribs,
a tenth share of his ashes in a smoked glass vial.

My eyes were riveted on a pin of light,
storm light, bare orchards, the heavens briefly
open: Emptied, ready to go —

One clear bee sputtering at the wet pane.

       Swipe of swift, aciculate claws.

2.

The torn swans were long syllables.
A breath of pine, and the woodsong fog.

Clear vowels rise like balloons:

I say moon is horses in the tempered dark.
I cry for no reason and plead with you.

What seas what shores what gray rocks
— the stones singing —

I speak because I am shattered, wrecked.

Your song, what does it know?
The moon swinging like a pendulum . . .
Me — of Me — ?

I answer that I cannot answer.
Not on my lips look for your mouth.

HOUSE-TREE-PERSON

*Projective test in which a subject's drawings are analyzed
for psychological significance.*

1. Heliotrope

When dark's hinged lid
closes, bend my
fingers round this spray —
dyers' crook —

this violet scent
my guide through starless
tropic. Perennial
verb, turn

your visage to
the vacanted sun. Many-
tongued, pray do
what I never — pray

do as I have done — yes
gather me
          sprig and stem

2. Passion Flower with Humble Plant

Milk-pink, passion's tendriled
corolla stretches
its limbs, refusing to be
contained —
          beneath it, the humble
plant in its sturdy earthen pot
whispers . . .

flight is nothing without restraint

there is beauty in both
the bound and the radial crown.

3. Conservatory

Like a chest — locked —
my breast's orchestral bellow
and beat. Glass sleeves
my hand and fist,

       breath's low
script a score — caesura —
silence's clear pour. By hand
and wrist I train the rows

of scripted vine, scores of
green — out of season
— the staked orchid an arrow
loose-planted in air —

out of season, this hot-house
beauty — locked
in air's breath-beaten glass:
loose-leaved — sheaved.

4. House-Tree-Person

The locked door — the window barred.

The great white all
that remains — my father's oaked arms.

Shrouded little forms. Muffled faces.

5. Untranslatable

The mourning lily's
black-veined face.

The unmown fields
I trespass

daily. The iris's slack-
jaw mouth. Ruffles

of blue lip webbed
by a spider's stintless

hours. The quiet.

6. Restoration

I will not re-leaf
unmarked by this my
season of alteration.

Swells of sweet
pea, my witching hazel,
I am nothing

you would recognize.
Unruly, I teem —
moth-powder and mouthless

— and velvet-blank
the little faces ghost
their old green galleries.

1. Exterior: Shutters

You know all of it: honeyed cell I settle
and claim for my own; *Draw the shades*; how gold-
dipped bees pulse luminescent; the molten
ring of sundrops round the dead; all I hold
dear; relentless industry, syllables
like so many spoonfuls of royal jelly —
you know it all. It's what you don't that is the trouble.

2. *Interior: Panel Left*

Apian forms bronzed like a baby's first shoes,
leather creases a burnished, metal love.
Isn't that the way. No other to show
what *to cherish* means, to hold mother's hard love
in my hands. Call me unfair — but how could
she fail to teach me to love, to flicker?
To claim my body's wick, its lit flame, its shiver?

3. Interior: Centerpiece

       In the catalog, a line of bees edge
scalloped bedsheets: the navy, garnet, or
dark gold? How to choose? Shudder of ledge
underfoot, I think queen-sized, I think dark
December hive, furred forms shifting. Patient.
I want to tuck my soul beneath my chin
and sleep, to survive this long Wisconsin winter.

4. Interior: Panel Right

Hammer and stamp me — I can handle more
than you know. Press hard, hand to my flesh's
unstruck page. A faint relief to the touch.
Watch how its violet ink must surface, this
body of mine an unlit lamp. Yes, mark
me in scrolls of sooted stars until I come
mirror-writ and humming, all I know of desire.

TO WINTER

after the painting by Giuseppe Arcimboldo, 1563

You are catch-less, you are my abandonment —
You are my very own sweet crone.

Timeless slab of ice and raw scrub, you empty me
　　　　to pitted fruit-stone, a sacrifice
To the green, green moon.

You stiffen, sexless as the whiskered ditch's roots,
　　　　the sink-holed lawn,
　　　　the pruned limbs — mere stumps.

You drain the lemon's pulp beneath its bitter rind.
You disclose the corded trunk's grizzle.

Absent desire, you are reduced to offshoot of silver
　　　　maple, its thrust from

the throat's barked lock.
Stasis: this flame unfanned. A fallow wake.

Too, you are the snow fleas that swarm each footfall.
You are the breath that winnows the snow's
　　　　hard-pack like petaled clouds.

Unplait me.

I want this for us:
both the re-leaf and release of furrowed brow and chest.
To feel the blossom of a lover's breath.

To feel you untie the knotted throat.

"A Frightful Release": The title and subtitles of "A Frightful Re-lease" are indebted to Gertrude Stein's *Tender Buttons*.

"Glass Armonica": The poems in this sequence center around notions of hysteria. Mary Glover's case is relevant in the history of the diagnosis because it was in relation to her case that Edward Jorden first produced a pamphlet spelling out the etiology and symptoms of "a disease called the Suffocation of the Mother"—in this interpretation, hysteria is the result of an afflicted uterus.

Franz Mesmer was also well known for his treatment of hysterics. He believed that through the manipulation of magnetic forces/fluid, he could heal his patients. Mesmer's most famous patient was the blind pianist, Maria Theresia Paradis, who—as a result of his "laying-on of hands"—announced that she could see.

The Salpêtrière hospital of Paris is notorious for having housed insane and incurable women patients, "hysterics." Under the direction of Dr. Jean-Martin Charcot, the inmates were photographed to provide evidence of hysteria's specific form and diagnostic criteria. One of Charcot's favorite cases, and among the most frequently photographed, was Augustine. She later escaped the Salpêtrière hospital, and lived out the rest of her life disguised as a man.

"Self-Portrait as He and She": For the phrasing in lines 7–8 and 13–15, I am indebted to an early draft of "love poem #29" by James Schiller.

"Learning to Pray" is a cento. Section 1 contains lines by my former teachers Scott Cairns, Eric Pankey, Debra Nystrom, Gerald Stern, Charles Wright, Jennifer Atkinson, Sherod Santos, Carolyn Forché, and Rita Dove, as well as ending with a translation by Sherod Santos. In section 2, lines are drawn from the following authors: Norman Dubie, T. S. Eliot, Sylvia Plath, Jack Gilbert, Anna Akhmatova, Louise Glück, Emily Dickinson, Marie Howe, Walt Whitman, and Paul Celan.

ACKNOWLEDGMENTS

Sincere thanks to all of the fellow writers who encouraged and in-
spired me while I was writing this book. Deepest gratitude to Milk-
weed Editions and G. C. Waldrep for bringing it into the world; and
to Aviva Cristy, Steve Gehrke, Mark Pioli, and James Schiller for
their rigorous and insightful guidance.

Thank you also to the University of Wisconsin–Milwaukee and the
Center for 21st Century Studies for fellowships that afforded me the
time to work on these poems, as well as to the editors of the literary
journals in which these poems first appeared:

Barrow Street: "Hemispherectomy"
Beloit Poetry Journal: "Restoration" and "Untranslatable"
Colorado Review: "Is Pear :: Is"
Connotation Press: "My Life as Narrated by Another" and
    "Self-Portrait as Phersu"
Crazyhorse: "Self-Portrait as Triptych" (as "Emblem")
CutBank: "The Garden of Earthly Delights"
Drunken Boat: "Ubi Sunt"
Meridian: "Melancholia as Invasive Species" and "Passion Flower
    with Humble Plant" (as part of "The Paper Garden")
Mudlark: "Self-Portrait as Convulsion," "Self-Portrait as
    Fragment," and "Self-Portrait as Cannibal"
Pembroke Magazine: "Conservatory"
RHINO: "Lines Written on the Margin of My Book"
So to Speak: "Glass Armonica"

Third Coast: "A Frightful Release" and "Pill"

TriQuarterly: "Stricken" (as "Insomnia Ghazal")

Valparaiso Poetry Review: "Rebecca"

Weave: "Heliotrope"

Several poems in the sequence "House-Tree-Person" appear in the chapbook, *Fascicle* (Dancing Girl Press, 2012).

REBECCA DUNHAM is the author of *The Miniature Room*, selected as winner of the 2006 T. S. Eliot Prize, and *The Flight Cage*, which was a Tupelo Press Open Reading Selection. She has also published a chapbook, entitled *Fascicle*. In 2005–06, Dunham was the Jay C. and Ruth Halls Fellow in Poetry at the Wisconsin Institute for Creative Writing, and in 2007 she received a National Endowment for the Arts fellowship. Dunham's poems have appeared widely in journals, including the *Iowa Review*, *Prairie Schooner*, *Crazyhorse*, *AGNI*, *Colorado Review*, *FIELD*, and the *Antioch Review*. She is a professor at the University of Wisconsin–Milwaukee, where she teaches in the creative writing program.

Interior design and typesetting by

Gretchen Achilles/Wavetrap Design

Typeset in Filosofia

MILKWEED EDITIONS

and

THE LINDQUIST & VENNUM FOUNDATION

are pleased to announce the second award of

THE LINDQUIST & VENNUM
PRIZE FOR POETRY

to

REBECCA DUNHAM

The annual, regional prize awards $10,000 and publication
by Milkweed Editions to a poet residing in North Dakota,
South Dakota, Minnesota, Iowa, or Wisconsin. The 2013
Lindquist & Vennum Prize for Poetry was judged
by G. C. Waldrep.

Established in 2011, the Lindquist & Vennum Prize for Poetry
celebrates poets for their artistic contributions and brings
outstanding regional writers to a national stage. Finalists
are selected from among all entrants by the editors of
Milkweed Editions. The winning collection is selected
annually by an independent judge.

Milkweed Editions is one of the nation's leading independent
publishers, with a mission to identify, nurture and publish
transformative literature, and build an engaged community
around it. The Lindquist & Vennum Foundation was
established by the Minneapolis-headquartered
law firm of Lindquist & Vennum, PLLP, and is a
donor-advised fund of The Minneapolis Foundation.